The **Science** and **Technology** of **BASKETBALL**

The **Science** and
Technology of
Sports

The Science and Technology of BASKETBALL

Bradley Steffens

ReferencePoint
Press®

San Diego, CA

© 2020 ReferencePoint Press, Inc.
Printed in the United States

For more information, contact:
ReferencePoint Press, Inc.
PO Box 27779
San Diego, CA 92198
www.ReferencePointPress.com

LIBRARY OF CONGRESS CATALOGING-IN-PUBLICATION DATA

Name: Steffens, Bradley, 1955– author.
Title: The Science and Technology of Basketball/by Bradley Steffens.
Description: San Diego, CA: ReferencePoint Press, Inc., [2020] | Series: The Science and Technology of Sports | Includes bibliographical references and index. | Audience: 9 to 12.
Identifiers: LCCN 2019004314 (print) | LCCN 2019009676 (ebook) | ISBN 9781682826508 (eBook) | ISBN 9781682826492 (hardback)
Subjects: LCSH: Basketball—Juvenile literature. | Sports sciences—Juvenile literature. | Sports—Technological innovations—Juvenile literature. Classification: LCC GV885.1 (ebook) | LCC GV885.1 .S72 2020 (print) | DDC 796.323—dc23
LC record available at https://lccn.loc.gov/2019004314

CONTENTS

Beyond Statistics

During a two-week period in the 2013 season, the Golden State Warriors of the National Basketball Association (NBA) found that opposing teams were making more three-point shots than usual against their defense. The Warrior coaches did not know how to fix the problem—because they did not know what was causing it. Desperate for a solution, they turned to Mocap Analytics, a company that provides computer analysis of basketball player locations on the court. Earlier in the season, the NBA had installed optical tracking cameras stationed at six points around the basketball arena to record the movements of every player and the ball twenty-five times a second throughout the game. The Mocap team scoured the optical tracking information and found small openings the Warriors players were leaving in their defense. "We were able to pinpoint the actions—and [Mocap] helped us do it—and understand the actions that led to that,"[1] said Golden State assistant general manager Kirk Lacob. Guided by the data, the Warriors were able to close the gaps in their defense and choke off the three-point shooting.

optical
Of or relating to vision: visual

A Revolution in Data Analytics

The NBA saw optical tracking systems as a way to help teams raise the quality of play and make the game more entertaining. The high-tech equipment can tell a coach things like which player is fastest, who dribbles the most compared to how many shots they take, who scores the most points per touch of the basketball, and where to find the best channels for attack. To ensure all teams benefited from the emerging technology, the NBA installed the optical tracking equipment in all NBA arenas in 2013. The NBA was the first professional sports league to make optical tracking systems available to its teams, but other professional leagues are following its lead. Aware that computer technology is always changing, the NBA hosts a "hackathon"—an event to demonstrate new technologies—once a year to encourage data scientists to present their innovations to the league.

Every NBA franchise now has a data analytics department in the front office, reviewing the optical tracking data and passing useful findings to the coaching staff. In a league in which games are often decided by a single point and one additional victory in a season can mean the difference between making the play-offs

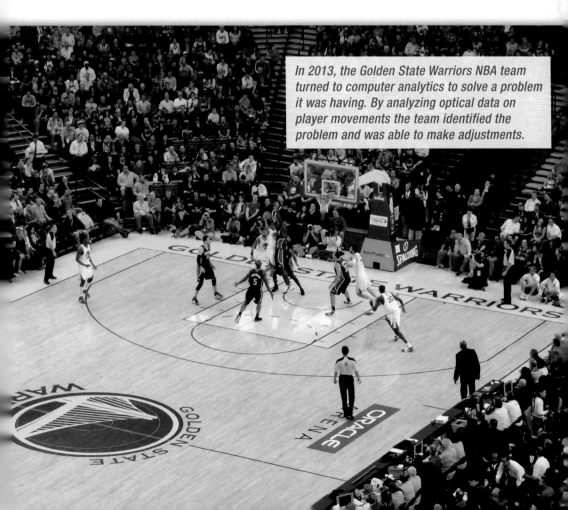

In 2013, the Golden State Warriors NBA team turned to computer analytics to solve a problem it was having. By analyzing optical data on player movements the team identified the problem and was able to make adjustments.

and going home, even the slightest tactical edge is important. The data analysts focus not only on the team they work for but also on the team's opponents, looking for weaknesses that can be exploited. Coaches use the computer data to design offensive plays that take advantage of a flaw in an opponent's defense and to juggle the lineup to create productive matchups with opposing players.

Beyond the Naked Eye

These data-driven adjustments are not always obvious. For example, a team might put a taller player into the game to create a mismatch against a smaller player. However, the opposing team's data analytics might say that the taller player moves better to one side than to the other. As a result, the countermove might not be to put in a taller player as well but rather to use a smaller player who excels at defending against the new player's preferred direction and can take advantage of the player's weakness when on offense. Detailed player profiles, not general statistics, determine which matchups are best for a team. "An organic approach to team performance, or an 'eye test,' used to be the norm," says Euan Hunter, an executive with Innovation Enterprise, a business media company. "This approach would see coaches formulate tactics based on gut instinct. This emergence of analytics, however, has changed this. Now, coaches pore over data points, using them to create game plans, and to map the most effective route to victory."[2]

The NBA's use of high-tech equipment extends beyond the games to the practice court, the gym, and even into the players' daily routines, all in an effort to raise the level of performance. At practice, players can wear electronic sensors attached to their shoes and play with a ball that also has an embedded sensor, allowing the data analytics team

sensor
An electronic device that detects or measures a physical property and records or otherwise responds to it

8

to map the activity in three dimensions. This equipment gives immediate feedback to the coaches and players, which enables them to adjust on the spot and makes practice more effective. In the gym, wearable sensors provide instant feedback on the biomechanics of physical efforts, such as running and jumping. Some players even wear lightweight waterproof sensors in their daily life to track their activity and monitor how quickly they recover from the exertion of games and practice, all in an attempt to reduce injuries and enhance their play.

biomechanics
The study of the movement of a living body

The professionals are not the only ones using technology to improve their play. College and high school basketball teams are also taking advantage of embedded sensors and other practice aids to improve their players' biomechanics; shooting, passing, and rebounding skills; and team play. Technology is revolutionizing basketball at all competitive levels.

CHAPTER ONE

The Biomechanics of Basketball

Golden State Warrior point guard Stephen Curry takes an outlet pass from teammate Draymond Green and dribbles into the front court against a lone defender for the Los Angeles Clippers, 6-foot-9-inch (205.7 cm) Danny Granger. Curry's teammate Steve Blake is flying down the left side of the court in a two-on-one fast break. Clippers guard Darren Collison is two steps behind Curry, hoping to disrupt the play. Curry watches Granger to see if he will sag back toward the basket to defend against a possible pass to Blake for an easy layup. When Granger glances at Blake, Curry plants his feet behind the three-point line, jumps, and shoots. Collison swipes at the ball, but it is already gone. Before the ball even reaches the basket, Curry is turning away. He knows it is going in, and it does.

This shot came against the Clippers, but it could have come against anyone. Curry has made more than twenty-three hundred three-point shots in his career and is on pace to break the NBA record for most career three-pointers. He already holds six NBA records for three-point shooting. "I love everything about shooting," says Curry, "but mostly that perfect form, when your body is in rhythm from the time you plant your feet to the time you release the ball. When it happens, everything is very smooth and calm from your feet through your release. Everything moves through you like a wave, almost. It's a beautiful thing."[3]

Only 6 feet 3 inches (191 cm) tall in a league where players average 6 feet 7 inches (201 cm), Curry has had to hone his technique in order to compete. He takes one thousand shots before every practice. On game day Curry shoots two- and three-point shots from seven stations around the court, moving from one station to the next only after making ten of thirteen shots. An hour before the game, he spends fifteen to thirty minutes performing a series of drills focused on ball handling, shooting with his left hand, and other skills.

A great deal of science stands behind Curry's drills and technique. These principles have emerged from the science of biomechanics, the study of the movement of a living body, including how muscles, bones, tendons, and ligaments work together to produce movement. Some scientists have studied physical movements involved in many sports, including running and jumping. Others have studied the biomechanics of specific basketball skills, including shooting.

The Biomechanics of Running

The most basic skill used in basketball is running. A basketball player does not have to be a champion sprinter, but speed is an asset. For example, on a fast break, when an offensive team races down the court before the defense is set, a player who is slow to the basket can be caught from behind and sometimes have his or her shot blocked. A fast player can stay ahead of a defender for an easy layup or dunk.

ground reaction force

In physics, and especially in biomechanics, the force of the ground pushing back against a person or other living thing making contact with it

To propel the body forward, an athlete performs a complex series of movements involving the feet, ankles, legs, torso, and even arms and head. In terms of physics, the runner employs Isaac Newton's third law of motion, which states that for every action, there is an equal and opposite reaction. In the case of running, the action is the runner pushing his or her foot against the ground. The reaction is the force of the ground pushing back against the foot, known as ground reaction force. This force propels the runner's body off the ground and forward. "Running is a series of little jumps," says Mike Reinold, the former head athletic trainer for the Boston Red Sox of Major League Baseball. "The rear leg has to propel the body forward. The stride leg has to absorb force."[4] The ground reaction force at the center of the foot is about 250 percent of the runner's body weight. Speed is the result of how much force the runner applies to the ground and how quickly the runner is able to repeat the motion, a process known as speed of gait.

The most basic skill used in basketball is running. A basketball player does not have to be a champion sprinter, but speed is an asset.

The speed of something in a given direction is known as velocity. It takes a sprinter about 164 feet (50 m) to reach his or her maximum velocity. Since a basketball court is only 94 feet (28.7 m) long, a basketball player is gaining speed, or accelerating, throughout a sprint down the court. Since the player starts at zero velocity, the greatest amount of acceleration occurs in the first stride. While there is not enough room for a basketball player to achieve full speed on the court, most athletes achieve 80 percent of their top speed in the first 66 feet (20 m) of a sprint.

As a runner accelerates, his or her strides become longer. While it would seem logical that lengthening the stride as much as possible will create the greatest speed, this turns out not to be true. If the striding leg is too far ahead of the runner's center of gravity, it actually acts as a brake when it hits the ground, with some of the ground reaction force traveling backward toward the runner's center of gravity.

velocity
The speed of something in a given direction

acceleration
The increase, or positive change, in speed over time

The Biomechanics of the One-Legged Jump

There are two kinds of jumps in basketball and other sports: one-legged jumps and two-legged jumps. In the one-legged jump, only one leg is in contact with the ground before the jump, a period known as ground support time. The two-legged jump has both legs in contact with the ground during this time.

The use of one jump rather than the other is partly the result of the game situation and partly the preference of the jumper. One-legged jumps are used by players moving forward who need to get up in the air quickly. Most of the time this jump is used by an offensive player who is driving toward the basket for a layup or dunk. A one-legged jump takes less than half a second (0.46 seconds) to execute, while a two-legged jump takes more than half a second (0.58). This difference of almost one-tenth of a second (.08 seconds) can mean the difference between getting the shot off and having it blocked.

One-legged jumps are occasionally used on defense when the player is sprinting from behind the offensive player and needs to quickly elevate to block the shot. For example, with the score tied 89–89 and just 1:52 remaining in game seven of the 2016 NBA championship series between the Cleveland Cavaliers and the Golden State Warriors, Andre Iguodala, a Warriors' guard, pulled down a rebound and started a two-on-one fast break. He passed to Warriors' guard Stephen Curry, who shot it back to Iguodala. Iguodala planted his left foot on the restricted zone line, 4 feet (1.2 m) from the basket, starting a one-legged jump to lay the ball in the basket. At the same time LeBron James, who was trailing the play, planted his left foot in the middle of the three-second lane and took off on his own one-legged jump. James sailed 7 feet (2.1 m) through the air, reached up at the highest point in his jump, and slammed Iguodala's layup into the backboard, denying the basket. "Superhuman defensive recovery by LeBron James,"[5] said former NBA player and coach and ESPN commentator Mark Jackson. James's effort, nicknamed "the Block" and "LeBlock," is considered one of the finest defensive plays of all time. Fifty-nine seconds later, the Cavaliers' Kyrie Irving made a three-point shot to give the Cavaliers the lead and the team's first NBA title in its forty-six year history.

momentum

The force of a moving object. The momentum of an object is equal to the mass of the object times the velocity of the object.

A one-legged jump involves blocking the forward, or horizontal, momentum and converting it into upward, or vertical, momentum, using ground reaction force. To accomplish this, the player stretches out the takeoff leg and plants it, causing the body to brake. Ideally, the forward leg is almost stiff, with a slight knee bend. The action is similar to the action of a track and field pole vaulter, in which the vaulter runs toward the

The Fastest Runners in the NBA

Since 2000 the NBA has tested the speed and agility of all new players who enter the league. According to the league's electronic timing equipment, only two players have run the test distance of three-fourths of the court in less than three seconds: Nate Robinson, a 5-foot-9-inch (175 cm) point guard who played eleven seasons in the NBA from 2005 to 2015, and Sonny Weems, a small forward who played for several NBA teams from 2008 to 2016. They both sprinted the distance in 2.96 seconds and are considered the fastest players in NBA history. All other NBA players who have participated in the three-quarters court sprint have clocked in at over 3 seconds, with the second-fastest being Donovan Mitchell of the Utah Jazz, at 3.01 seconds.

Speed in a sprint and speed in a game are two different things, however. John Wall, a point guard for the Washington Wizards, was clocked at 3.14 seconds in the NBA sprint, but his coach, Scott Brooks, believes he is the fastest NBA player of all time. "He is as fast as anybody in this league, and probably in the [league's] history—his speed, and his speed with the ball," Brooks says. "He's one of the best I've ever seen going at a full speed being able to see the other nine players on the court at the same time. . . . Not a lot of guys can do that."

Quoted in Chris Lingebach, "Brooks: John Wall Might Be Fastest Player in NBA History," CBS DC, October 26, 2016. https://washington.cbslocal.com.

---

bar and then plants the pole in the ground, converting the horizontal momentum into vertical momentum.

The jumper adds to the horizontal momentum by flexing and then straightening joints and muscles. The jumper's foot is planted flat on the ground so the jumper can use the foot muscles to push up, through the ball of the foot. The ankle is flexed forward before takeoff and then straightened during the jump. For maximum efficiency, the player's center of gravity, at about the level of the hips, must be kept low, and the chest should be lowered toward the knees prior to the jump. The straightening of the knee, hips, and torso during the jump add to the upward momentum. In addition, the trailing leg swings up, as if the player is taking a giant stride in the air, adding to the vertical momentum of the body.

Two-Legged Jumps

With 7:52 left in the first game of the 2013 season for the Women's National Basketball Association's (WNBA) Phoenix Mercury, Phoenix forward Charde Houston drove toward the basket. Two defenders from the opposing team, the Chicago Sky, moved toward her to guard against a possible shot. Houston dished the ball to Brittney Griner, the Mercury center, who was open in the lane. Without dribbling, Griner leaped up and dunked the

The two-legged jump involves more flexion and straightening of feet, ankles, knees, hips, and torso than the one-legged jump does.

ball. Five minutes later, Griner intercepted a crosscourt pass, drove to the basket, and dunked again. In her first game in the WNBA, Griner became only the third player in the league's history to dunk during a regular season game, and she had tied Candace Parker's record for most dunks in a career, with two. Griner has gone on to dunk a total of thirteen times, which is five more than the rest of the league combined. At 6 feet 8 inches (203 cm) tall, Griner uses a two-legged jump to get her hands high enough above the rim to dunk. Of the seven WNBA players to have dunked during a game, she is the only one to use a two-legged takeoff.

Like one-legged jumps, two-legged vertical jumps rely on ground reaction force. When Griner pushes against the ground with her feet, the ground reaction force propels her into the air. Sometimes Griner, like other players, converts horizontal momentum into vertical momentum by taking a forward hop before the two-legged jump. Other times the two-legged jump is made from a stationary or almost stationary position. Two-legged jumps are used on offense, especially to execute jump shots and dunks. They are also used on defense to defend against and sometimes block shots.

The two-legged jump involves more flexion and straightening of feet, ankles, knees, hips, and torso than the one-legged jump does. Because of the deeper flexion, the two-legged jump takes longer to execute than a single-leg jump does, but it also results in a higher jump for most athletes. In addition, more athletes are able to execute a two-legged jump consistently than a one-legged jump, because the approach and timing is simpler.

The Jump Shot

The two-legged jump is employed during the most popular basketball shot, the jump shot. Jump shots make up about 70 percent of all shots taken in a basketball game. Since scoring is essential to winning basketball games, the jump shot is one of the most studied of all movements used in basketball.

There are two kinds of jump shot: the two-part jump shot and the one-part jump shot. The two-part jump shot is more common. In the first part of the shot, the shooter creates a triangle by bending deeply at the shoulder, hip, and knee. In the second part, the player explodes upward, raises the ball, and releases it near the top of the jump. In the one-part shot, the shooter does not bend deeply before takeoff and does not wait to reach to the top of the jump to release the ball. Instead, the shooter releases the ball on the way up. As a result, the one-part shot takes less time to execute. Stephen Curry has one of the quickest one-part shots in NBA history. It takes him just four-tenths of a second to execute his shot, while the average NBA player takes six-tenths of a second to execute a two-part jump shot. The two-tenths of a second that Curry saves with his one-part shot gives him extra time to shoot before a defender can close in on him. His shot is so quick that by six-tenths of a second, when a two-part shooter is just releasing the ball, Curry's ball has already traveled 12 feet (3.7 m) toward the basket.

The Arms and Hands During the Shot

Despite the differences in lower body motion, the one-part and two-part jump shots are virtually identical above the waist—the player aims and releases the ball. There are many ways to shoot the basketball, but in the classic jump shot, the shooter lifts the ball as he or she jumps and raises it slightly above eye level. The shooting arm is held in front of the body, with the upper arm—from the shoulder to the elbow—pointing toward the basket, not out to the side. The elbow is bent at a 90 degree angle so the forearm is straight up and down. The forearm is also in line with the basket. The shooter's wrist is rotated so the back of the wrist faces the shooter and the heel of the hand faces the basket. The shooting hand is bent backward at the wrist at a 90 degree angle, making a flat resting place for the ball. The position of the hand and arm is similar to that of a waiter carrying a tray of food above his or her head. The ball rests in the palm and fingers of the shooting hand.

In the classic jump shot, the shooter lifts the ball as he or she jumps and raises it above eye level. The elbow is bent at a 90 degree angle so the forearm is straight up and down.

The nonshooting hand does little other than keep the ball stationary until just before the ball is released. Curry says he keeps his nonshooting hand "paralyzed" to avoid affecting the launch of the ball in any way. Depending on the player's wrist strength and the distance to the basket, the shooter might bend his or her forearm back, beyond 90 degrees, to launch the ball with more power, like a catapult. Ideally, the shooter's elbow, forearm, wrist, and hand

Best Leapers in Professional Basketball

The NBA player with the greatest vertical jump is Michael Jordan, who was nicknamed "Air Jordan" for his leaping ability. Jordan's vertical jump was 48 inches (122 cm). This put the top of Jordan's head 6 inches (15.2 cm) above the 10-foot-high (3 m) rim. Jordan—who holds the NBA records for highest career regular season scoring average (30.12 points per game) and highest career play-off scoring average (33.45 points per game)—jumped higher than renowned current players LeBron James of the Los Angeles Lakers (44 inches, or 112 cm) and Vince Carter of the Atlanta Hawks (43 inches, or 109 cm).

Jordan's vertical leap was an incredible 20 inches (51 cm) higher than the NBA average. Only Darrell Griffith, who played for the Utah Jazz from 1981 to 1993, has recorded a vertical jump of 48 inches (122 cm). Anthony "Spud" Webb is next highest, with a vertical jump of 46 inches (117 cm). Because of his leaping ability, Webb could dunk the ball even though he is only 5 feet 7 inches (171 cm) tall. In fact, Webb won the NBA's 1986 Slam Dunk Contest with a series of spectacular dunks.

The greatest Maximum Vertical Leap recorded by the NBA since it began testing rookie players in 2000 belongs to Kenny Gregory, who leaped 45.5 inches (116 cm) in 2001. Second highest is Hamidou Diallo, a guard with the Oklahoma Thunder, who jumped 44.5 inches (113 cm) in 2017. Diallo's amazing leaping ability helped him win the NBA's 2019 Slam Dunk Contest.

are all stacked in one vertical line. This alignment of the entire arm with the basket will keep the shot on line toward the target when it is released.

To propel the ball toward the basket, the arm straightens at the elbow, and then the wrist straightens. As the wrist straightens, the ball, which was cradled in the palm of the hand, is propelled forward, rolling off the shooter's fingertips. Unlike the elbow, which goes from 90 degrees of flexion to straight, the hand continues moving after the shot to a full 180 degrees and even beyond, from flexed backward to flexed forward in a "gooseneck" finish—the arm and hand position resembling the neck and head of a goose.

In biomechanical terms, the shooting hand and arm function as levers. A lever is a rigid bar that is used to move an object. A teeter-totter is a type of lever. It consists of a rigid bar balanced on another object in the middle, known as the pivot or fulcrum. When force is applied downward to one end of the teeter-totter, known as the effort end, the other end, known as the load end, rises. This simple machine can be used to move an object with less effort than is required by lifting it directly. When the fulcrum is located between the effort end and the load end, as in a teeter-totter, that is a known as first-class lever.

A different kind of lever, known as a third-class lever, works in a similar way. In a third-class lever, the load is at one end, and the fulcrum is at the other. The force is applied between the two ends. A broom is a third-class lever. The bristles are the load end. The hand at the top end of the broom is the fulcrum. The force is applied by the other hand to the middle of the broom, moving the lever to sweep.

During the basketball shot, the forearm functions as a third-class lever. The hand with the ball is the load, and the elbow is the fulcrum. A muscle known as the triceps applies force to the center of the forearm, like a hand on the center of a broom. This moves the hand and ball forward, pivoting on the elbow.

The hand and wrist also work as a third-class lever. Again, the hand and ball are the load. The wrist is the fulcrum. Muscles in the forearm apply force to the center of the hand, snapping it forward and propelling the ball through the air.

The beauty of a basketball shot is obvious to all. Watching a 9-inch (23 cm) ball arc 30 feet (9 m) through the air and into a hoop just 18 inches (46 cm) across can be thrilling. The mechanics underlying it all are not as obvious, but are just as elegant—a linked and synced system of levers that work together to send a projectile in an exact direction, at a precise angle, at the perfect speed to fall untouched through the targeted space.

CHAPTER TWO

Mapping the Game

Statistical analysis has been used for decades in all professional sports to enhance team performance. Most of these changes were simple. For example, facing a basketball team with an outstanding scorer, a coach might insert a defensive specialist into the lineup in hopes of lowering the star shooter's point production and forcing the opposing team to rely on its other players for scoring. Similar tactics are even more prevalent in baseball, where one-on-one matchups occur on every play, when a hitter faces a pitcher. For example, since left-handed hitters generally perform better against right-handed pitchers than right-handed hitters do, managers often insert as many left-handed players into the lineup as possible against a right-handed pitcher, and vice-versa for left-handed pitchers.

The Coming of Analytics

These kinds of strategies were taken to a new level in the early 2000s, when the Oakland Athletics baseball team began to use computers to analyze statistics in a new way. This technique was documented in the book and later the movie *Moneyball*—a term that is now associated with the science of statistics-based predictive analysis in all sports. *Moneyball* revealed a deeper understanding of pitcher-hitter matchups as well as the likely success of certain strategies in a given situation. Teams using statistical

predictive analysis
The practice of extracting information from existing data sets in order to determine patterns and predict future outcomes and trends

Predictive analysis of statistics was not as helpful in basketball as it was in other sports such as baseball. Basketball is a fluid game and does not present the static situations and matchups that baseball does.

predictive analysis, including the Athletics, enjoyed great success. As a result, the technique has been adopted by a wide range of professional sports, including soccer, football, and basketball.

Predictive analysis based on statistics was not as helpful in basketball as it was in other sports, however. This is because the moneyball approach analyzes certain situations that have defined starting and ending points—known as states—to find the most probable outcome. Basketball, however, is fluid game and does not present the static situations and matchups that baseball does.

Plotting Every Shot

One of the first people to realize the limitations of statistical analysis was Kirk Goldsberry, currently the vice president of strategic research for the San Antonio Spurs. An amateur basketball player and a geography professor who worked on real-time traffic maps, Goldsberry believed that basketball analytics was essentially a mapping challenge—a matter of tracking where players were when certain things happened on the court.

Goldsberry used public data published by ESPN to identify the locations of every shot taken in the NBA from 2006 to 2011—more than seven hundred thousand of them. He plotted these shots, player by player, on a computer-generated map of a basketball court that resembles a video game screen. Using these maps, Goldsberry could show how many shots each NBA player took from each location on the floor and how many of those shots were made.

Goldsberry used five different-sized circles to represent the frequency of shots a player took from a particular location—small for few shots through large for many. He then color coded the circles to represent the player's scoring percentage from that location—from dark blue at the low end through yellow and orange in the middle to red at the high end. The result was an easy-to-read "signature" of each player's effectiveness from every inch of the 1,284-square-foot (119.3 sq. m) area from which players take almost all of their shots.

The results of the mapping, which Goldsberry called CourtVision, were surprising. For example, they showed that Dirk Nowitzki, the 7-foot (213 cm) power forward for the Dallas Mavericks, takes about the same number of shots from every position on the court but is most effective in two places—under the basket, which was not a surprise, but also behind the three-point line, which was. These maps are used to design plays to get the shooter an open shot from the spot on the court where he has the greatest chance of success.

Optical Tracking

Goldsberry's mapping was innovative but still static. It showed what had happened but not why. However, basketball analytics took a leap forward when Goldsberry teamed up with a company called STATS to analyze data from the company's optical tracking

Optical tracking analysis helped teams determine which players defended best against shots taken near the basket. Dwight Howard (in red) of the Washington Wizards is one of the best NBA players in this metric.

system called SportVU. Originally developed by the Israeli army to track enemy missiles, SportVU cameras track every object on the court, from the players to the ball to the referees, twenty-five times a second. Player and referee positions are extracted from the data and plotted in two-dimensional maps, while the ball location is plotted in three dimensions. This data allowed analysts to track things that had never been looked at before, such as dribbles, scores per touch of the basketball, and a defensive player's position on the court throughout a play and the impact it has on the outcome of the play. "We can, for the first time, create topological networks of the players in the NBA which will allow us for the first time, with mathematical rigor, to discover the positions, the true positions, of basketball,"[6] observed data analyst Muthu Alagappan.

topological
Of or relating to the way in which constituent parts are interrelated or arranged

"Ghost Players"

Most NBA teams use data analytics to see what happened in a game or what is happening in real time. However, one team, the Toronto Raptors, is using it to show what the team should do in the future to be more effective.

The Raptors' data analytics team converted optical tracking data into a map of player positions, represented by colored dots—white for the Raptors and blue for their opponents—with the players' numbers on the dots. The team animated the moment-to-moment diagrams of player positions to show how the Raptor defense responded to a particular play, almost like watching a video game. "In simple terms: the Raptors' analytics team wrote insanely complex code that turned all those X-Y coordinates from every second of every recorded game into playable video files," says NBA broadcaster Zach Lowe.

The data analytics team then used computers to identify similar situations in other games that resulted in defensive stops. They used machine learning programming to identify the ideal movements to counter the attack by the opposing team. These movements were overlaid onto the video files as a third group of dots—transparent circles with the Toronto players' numbers on them—to represent where the players should have been to better defend the play. "Those are ghost players," says Lowe, "and they are doing what Toronto's coaching staff and analytics team believe the players should have done on this play." The real players then mimic the ghost movements to improve their defensive play.

Quoted in Dan Peterson, "Learning from Ghosts—How AI and Machine Learning Are Changing Sports," *The 80 Percent Mental Blog*, January 19, 2018. www.80percentmental.com.

Again, the results were surprising. Before optical tracking, defensive analysis focused on how many shots a player blocked or how many steals the player had. Goldsberry could tell finer things. He could tell which defensive players were best at reducing the opponent's shooting percentages within a 5-foot (1.5 m) radius of the basket, where most points are scored. He was also able to determine which players reduced the total number of shots taken in this area. The leader in this metric was Dwight Howard of the Washington Wizards. Goldsberry found that Howard caused teams to take 9 percent fewer shots around the basket, leading to fewer baskets made and more wins for his team.

Six NBA teams installed SportVU in their arenas during the 2010–2011 season and began to record their games. By the 2012–2013 season, fifteen NBA teams were using SportVU. Wanting to give all teams the same chance to compete, the NBA placed SportVU cameras in all thirty NBA arenas for the 2013–2014 season. The "NBA has been one of the most forward-looking leagues in terms of technology, in terms of being on top of new innovations in tech," says Courtney Brunious, the associate director of the University of Southern California Sports Business Institute. "As a whole, I would say the NBA is probably the most tech-savvy amongst the leagues."[7] Beginning in the 2016–2017 season, the NBA replaced SportVU with Second Spectrum, a system that combines video tracking with data analytics.

data analytics
The science of examining data sets to draw conclusions about the information they contain, often with the aid of specialized systems and software

How Technology Is Changing the Game

Data analytics has already changed the NBA. The most obvious change is the use of the three-point shot. A holdover from the old American Basketball Association, which introduced the long-range shot in 1967 as a way to add excitement to its games, the three-pointer was a relative rarity in the NBA, with an average of only 2.8 three-point shots attempted per game five years after the shot was introduced into the league in 1979. In the 2017–2018 season, the NBA averaged more than ten times that amount—29 three-point shots per game. Data analytics has revealed that the three-point shot is a more potent weapon than the midrange two-point shot. As a result, the number of three-point shots taken has risen more than 50 percent in the years since the NBA began to use video tracking and data analytics. In

2015 NBA teams attempted more three-pointers than midrange two-pointers for the first time in history.

Some of the changes inspired by data analytics are more subtle. For example, in the 2018–2019 season, Los Angeles Clippers coach Doc Rivers introduced a new offense built around Second Spectrum maps of his players' shooting efficiency by location. The data suggested that the Clippers shooters should utilize a play known as the pick-and-roll. In a pick-and-roll, one player stands to the side of the opposing team's player defending the ball handler, creating a potential obstruction, known as a pick or screen. The ball handler then dribbles in the direction of the pick, causing the defender to slow down or stop because of the obstructing player. The ball handler either shoots from the opening created by the pick or passes to the player who set the pick as he or she moves, or "rolls," toward the basket. In the Clippers offense, Tobias Harris is usually the ball handler, and the picks are set by Marcin Gortat or Montrezl Harrell. During the 2018–2019 season, Harris was the ball handler on sixteen pick-and-rolls per game—twice as many as the year before. As a result, the team's true shooting percentage soared from tenth in the league to fourth. More importantly, the team's winning percentage improved from .512 to .585, or from eighteenth in the league to tenth. In addition, Harrell—the player rolling off many of the picks—is ranked second in the NBA in effective field goal percentage, a measurement of shooting percentage adjusted for the fact that three-point shots are worth 50 percent more (one point) than two-point shots. Harrell is ahead of such superstars as Kevin Durant, Klay Thompson, Kyrie Irving, Stephen Curry, and LeBron James in this shooting category.

Insights into Individual Players

Optical tracking and the accompanying data analytics reveal unappreciated aspects of players' games, even well-known players like James Harden of the Houston Rockets. Harden led the NBA in scoring in 2017–2018 and 2018–2019. Optical tracking reveals that Harden is scoring many of his points by going one-on-one with defenders in what is known as an isolation play. Harden is averaging 17.7 isolation plays, or ISOs, per game, which is 7 more per game than the player with the second most, DeMar DeRozan. The reason is simple: Harden's ISOs yield an average of 1.16 points each. This compares to just 0.99 points per offensive possession (not counting fast breaks) by the league's best scoring offense, the Milwaukee Bucks.

The way Harden succeeds with these ISOs is unique. He makes far more unassisted three-point shots than anyone in the league. An unassisted shot is one in which the player makes the basket on his or her own, not directly off a pass. In the NBA, 80 percent of three-point baskets come off assists. This is because many three-point shooters are catch-and-shoot experts who plant their feet behind the three-point line and line up with the basket before receiving the ball. For example, Klay Thompson and Kyle Korver

Optical tracking helped reveal that James Harden of the Houston Rockets makes far more unassisted three-point shots than anyone in the league.

make more than 90 percent of their three-point shots off assists. By contrast, only 15 percent of Harden's three-pointers are set up by an assist. In the 2017–2018 season, Harden set a league record by making 196 unassisted three-point shots. In 2019, he shattered his own record with 317 unassisted three-pointers.

In his unassisted three-pointers, Harden works his defender out of position by dribbling before taking his shot—often a "step back" jump shot, in which Harden takes a long step away from the basket and the defender before launching the shot. Second Spectrum data reveals that an average Harden three-pointer is preceded by 8.4 dribbles. By contrast, the average NBA three-pointer is preceded by only 1.14 dribbles. Stephen Curry takes an average of 1.99 dribbles before launching his three-pointer. Harden dribbles more than any other player in the NBA, according to Second Spectrum data.

When Harden does not step back and shoot, he often drives to the basket and draws a foul. This, too, is by design. Harden has led the league in free throws every year since the 2014–2015 season. When Harden goes to the free throw line to shoot a pair of free throws, he scores an average of 1.7 points. An average NBA possession (including fast breaks) is worth 1.1 points, so Harden's foul strategy is sound. When Harden does not shoot, he often dishes the ball to Rockets center Clint Capela. The Harden-to-Capela play has resulted in more baskets and is the second-most efficient passer-to-shooter connection in the NBA, according to Second Spectrum data.

Some people find Harden's ISOs and dribbling boring compared to the fast passing of teams like the San Antonio Spurs and Golden State Warriors. "Love him or hate him, Harden is the most fascinating player in the world right now," observes data analytics pioneer Goldsberry. "[Houston head coach Mike] D'Antoni has engineered simple but brutally effective sets that give his star the most chances to shine."[8] It is an offense guided by Second Spectrum tracking and data analytics. While the average NBA half-court possession is worth .99 points, or slightly less than 1 point,

Optical Tracking in the National Collegiate Athletic Association

STATS SportVU, the first optical tracking system used by the NBA, is affordable enough to be used by some college basketball programs. Indiana University, which has won five National Collegiate Athletic Association (NCAA) basketball national championships, contracted with STATS to install SportVU cameras above the university's basketball court. The cameras will track players' movements during home games. Clif Marshall, the Hoosiers' director of athletic performance, was particularly interested in analyzing the players' fitness to help maximize their performance during games. STATS analyzed the SportVU data and produced reports on players' speed on the court, the distance they covered during the games, and their average jump heights. Marshall gives credits to the system for the steady progress the athletes made over three years. "We broke it down for our players—this was your max speed three years ago, this is where you were at two years ago and this is where you're at now," Marshall says. "And for almost every player, they had gotten faster. Showing them that data is really important."

Quoted in STATS, "Indiana Hoosiers Maximize Player Performance with STATS SportVU," 2018. http://docs.stats.com.

Harden's averages for three-point shooting and free throws are all greater than 1 point. On average, his three-point shot is worth 1.12 points, his two-point foul is worth 1.73 points, and his three-point shooting foul is worth 2.60 points. The moneyball offense built around Harden works. The Rockets have won their division twice since 2014 and made the play-offs in all seven seasons that Harden has been with team.

Using Data to Entertain the Fans

Some NBA executives see more in Second Spectrum than a way to elevate play. They see it as a way for the fans to be entertained by the game and, as a result, more loyal to the team and league. In the 2018–2019 season, the Los Angeles Clippers and Second

Spectrum teamed up to create Clippers Court Vision, a digital enhancement system for watching games on television. The service uses Second Spectrum data and computer animation to add relevant information to the broadcast. The idea was to create real-time visuals similar to the computer-generated graphics used to show the strike zone in televised baseball or the first-down line in televised football. In "player" mode, the CourtVision viewer can watch the action from a point guard's point of view, looking down the court. As the offensive players move around the court, their effective shooting percentage hovers above their heads, along with a matching bar graph that is color coded—green for a high percentage, orange for a middle percentage, and red for a low percentage. The colors and numbers show which players are open for the most effective shots. In "coach" mode, the system uses machine learning and advanced graphics to diagram plays on the floor as they happen. In "fan" mode, the viewer sees fun graphics such as a computer-animated lightning bolt striking and electrifying the backboard and rim when a player makes a three-point shot.

The NBA's optical tracking system is still in its infancy, as is the data analytics used to make sense of the information. As techniques become more refined, the insights will shape how the game is played, which players see more playing time, and even which players are drafted into the professional leagues. The game will continue to evolve.

CHAPTER THREE

Making Practice More Effective

Basketball teams spend a great deal of time practicing. Practice is where players hone their skills and teams develop their plays and strategies. Games are not won in practice, but they can be lost there. "Failing to prepare is preparing to fail,"[9] said John Wooden, the one-time head coach at the University of California–Los Angeles, whose teams won ten NCAA national championships in a twelve-year period. To prepare, coaches need to make practice as efficient and effective as possible, especially in high school and college, when students have limited availability for practice. As a result, coaches are increasingly using technology to focus practices on the things that will most improve individual players as well as the team.

Tracking Systems

With the license for a Second Spectrum optical tracking system costing more than $1 million a year, few if any amateur basketball programs can afford the state-of-the-art player tracking equipment. However, there are lower-cost systems that are capable of tracking players and the ball in real time. STATS SportVU, the first optical tracking system used by the NBA, costs about $100,000 a year, which puts it within budget for elite college basketball programs. In 2013 perennial NCAA basketball power Duke University became the first to install SportVU equipment, but it was soon followed by the

University of Louisville and Marquette University. The teams use the cameras and the statistical information they provide in their playing arenas and in their practice facilities. "Our proprietary work with SportVU provides us a more complete picture of each player on our team and puts us in a stronger position to further their development," says Kevin Cullen, basketball director of information technology at Duke. "The insights we've made these first two years have been invaluable, and we believe we are just getting started."[10]

Another option for tracking player movements is ShotTracker. Rather than using multiple high-speed cameras to track actions on the court, ShotTracker employs radio frequency identification trackers that are attached to the players' shoes and are embedded in the ball. Each tracker sends a signal to sensors mounted in the rafters above the court. The above-court sensors relay the location data to computers, which then use the information to map the positions of the players and the ball. ShotTracker is much less expensive than optical tracking systems, so amateur teams can afford it.

Like optical tracking systems, sensor-based systems can show the locations of each player's shot attempts during practice and identify which shots are made and which are missed. This might sound basic, but it is not. Practice facilities are typically designed with a full court and two small courts crossing it at each end, for a total of six half-court areas. During practice, players often are shooting at all six baskets at once. Tracking what each player does at each of the six baskets is ex-

ShotTracker electronic basketballs sit on chargers during a college basketball game. The ShotTracker system is much less expensive than optical tracking systems, so amateur teams can afford it.

tremely difficult without the data analytics. Typically, coaches focus on what is happening at one or two baskets, usually where the starting players are practicing. As a result, they can miss when a second- or third-string player is shooting well. Most programs have student managers take notes on clipboards, recording shots, rebounds, and other statistics at all baskets and then developing reports after the practice is over. "We just weren't efficient at all," says Thomas Montigel, director of basketball operations at Texas Christian University, one of the colleges that switched from manual systems to ShotTracker.

> There were four student managers sitting at a table, heads down, tallying up stats, and a senior manager following the action, basically live-directing. So, "#10 just took a shot. Missed two. #1 got the rebound. Pass to #10." Then they'd spend hours in the office breaking it down into analytics and organizing it into documents.[11]

Magic Johnson Touts Player Tracking for Practice

Wearable player tracking devices have been adopted by some professional teams for use during practice. One of those teams is the Los Angeles Lakers. Earvin "Magic" Johnson, who as the point guard of the Lakers led the team to five NBA championships and is now president of operations for the Lakers, is a big advocate of using player tracking data during practice. In a panel discussion at the 2018 NBA All-Star Technology Summit, Johnson told the audience:

They can track, in real time, in practice, where the guys shoot well from, where they don't shoot well from. There would be a young man or a young lady collecting that data. They can tell coach Walton, "Hey, today, the guy was five for fifteen from the field. He probably needs to work on his corner three-pointer or his midrange game, or whatever it is." So in real time, we get that information, even if we call a time-out in practice, he can go and get that data right there, and that's really going to help our team, whether that's in practice or in games.

Quoted in ShotTracker, "Magic Johnson Talks ShotTracker," 2018. https://shottracker.com.

Using the mapping technology, the coaches can get all of the statistics automatically, both during and after practice. The tracking system gives every player an equal chance of being recognized for a strong practice. This encourages all players to do their best all the time, since their activities are always being recorded.

Player tracking systems can generate a color-coded map for each player, showing that player's strongest and weakest shooting areas during practice. Coaches can then create drills to help the player improve shooting from his or her weak areas. At the same time, coaches can design plays that end up with the player taking the shot from his or her most productive location, or "heat zone." For example, if a forward shoots well from the right side of the free throw line, the coach could design a play to have a guard set a screen so the forward can come up from the baseline area and receive a pass at the preferred shooting spot. If a guard shoots well from the same spot, a play could be designed to have a forward set a screen so the guard can dribble past and shoot from the preferred area. In other words, computerized maps allow coaches to tailor plays to the strengths of each player instead of design plays that force players to shoot from areas of the floor where they are not productive, increasing the odds that the player will make the shot both in practice and in the game.

Player tracking systems automatically record more than seventy separate statistics, including shooting, dribbling, passing, steals, blocked shots, and more. This can reveal surprising statistics that make practice more effective. For example, the system might reveal that a particular player is an effective three-point shooter off a pass but not off the dribble. Conversely, another player might shoot better off the dribble. With this data, coaches can design plays that take advantage of individual player strengths, rather than just create generic openings for generic players.

The Mental Game

Computerized maps also give coaches credibility when they speak with their players. One of the most important things a coach must do is gain the confidence and trust of each player, especially when discussing what a player needs to do to improve. This can be difficult because many athletes, being competitive by nature, are slow to admit weaknesses in their play. By showing the player the data analytics captured by the tracking system, the coach can gain the player's trust more quickly than by offering what the player might construe as merely an opinion. Montigel explains:

> We've got this kid on our team, one of the best shooters in the Big 12, but almost every single time he'd shoot a 3-pointer, his toe would be on the line. You could add 100 points throughout the season for all the long 2's he'd take. Didn't matter how many times we'd tell him—your

toe was on the line—he wouldn't believe us. Now we have proof! "You really only made ten 3's, because the other 25 you made were long 2's." When kids can see it for themselves, nine times out of ten they're going to use it as motivation.[12]

By showing how data analytics guides coaching decisions and advice, a coach can gain a player's trust more quickly than by offering what the player might construe as merely an opinion.

Real-time data analytics can interact with the competitive nature of players in another way. Coaches have found that when players are shown statistics in real time—on a large monitor, for example—they are often motivated to raise their game and outperform their teammates. It becomes a competition: Who can make the most three-pointers during practice? Who can have the highest shooting percentage? Montigel says:

> Every kid wants to see their individual stats. And these kids are tech-savvy, always on their phones. They want instant gratification. So the PLAYER app delivers three things they really care about. Our guys are super-competitive. They're looking at their teammates' stats, saying stuff in the locker room like, "You had six turnovers, but I only had one." Then they're hitting the gym at night, going back to their buddies in the dorms and saying, "Hey, I just made 50 out of a hundred." It's a constant competition, which is obviously great for the team.[13]

Accountability

Coaches can also use the system to see who is practicing on their own time and how effective they are. This is important in programs that limit the time coaches can be with their players. For example, Division II women's basketball rules state that coaches cannot be present to instruct players during summer sessions. However, in 2018 Northwood University in Michigan became the first Division II school to install sensors and analytics to automatically track a player's progress. "ShotTracker is super-beneficial from our players' standpoint," says Northwood head coach Jeff Curtis. "Now they know where they need to focus their attention, based on the

turnover
In basketball, an instance of a team losing possession of the ball to the opposing team before a player takes a shot at his or her team's basket

data that they get. Our players have become a lot more interested in getting into the gym. They don't have to track shots manually in a notebook anymore. ShotTracker gives them more freedom to get a really good workout in."[14]

Automated tracking systems also hold players accountable for their practice habits. The system can track who is practicing and for how long. "The players have 24/7 access to the gym and the sensors are in our locker room," says Curtis. "We put a lot of emphasis on getting more shots up outside of practice, and this is going to be the monster in the closet, saying 'We know what you've been doing so don't come in here talking about playing time if you haven't put the time in.'"[15]

A Recruiting Tool

Although player tracking and analytics have been used in the NBA for only a few short years, there are already players who have grown up with data analytics in basketball. This is one of the main reasons coaches should embrace the technology, according to Mike Brey, the head men's basketball coach at the University of Notre Dame. "My advice to any young coaches starting out is: 'If you don't have a feel for the analytic world and how to work it into your program, hire someone who does, because it's very, very important moving forward,'" says Brey. "And maybe the most important reason is because our young people, our players are already into it, and they're already analyzing themselves through analytics."[16]

Because players are aware of analytics, schools that have them have an edge in recruiting. For example, a Division I women's basketball player was considering transferring to Northwood, a Division II school. Part of Curtis's pitch to the player was that Northwood was the only Division II school with sensor-based tracking for basketball. "Every single recruit we've talked to has been really impressed that we have this technology in our gym. It gives them the sense that we're going to do everything we can to get a com-

Women Are Better Free Throw Shooters than Men Are

Analyzing data over a thirty-year period, basketball analytics experts Larry M. Silverberg and Chau Tran discovered that female college basketball players are better free throw shooters than male players are. In a study published in December 2018, Silverberg and Tran found that women shoot at 3 percent higher consistency than men.

Silverberg and Tran focused their study on NCAA athletes, whose average free throw shooting percentage has been around 68 percent for both men and women for more than thirty years. They factored in the differences between the men's and women's equipment. The men's ball is slightly larger than the women's ball, making the free throw more difficult, but the women's ball has more bounce, making it harder to get favorable bounces into the basket. Men are on average taller than women, giving them a higher release point and easier shot.

Silverberg and Tran decided that "the better sex would be determined by the one who is the most consistent, taking into account the physical differences between basketball size and the height at which the ball is released." They looked at these criteria across millions of simulated shots. "When we looked at the data this way, we saw that the standard deviations for the women were about 3 percent smaller than for the men, taking into account physical differences in basketball size and average player's height," writes Silverberg. "In other words, on average, women need to be 3 percent more consistent than men to achieve their average shooting percentages reported by the NCAA."

Larry M. Silverberg, "Women Are Better than Men at the Free Throw Line," The Conversation, January 23, 2019. https://theconversation.com.

petitive advantage," says Curtis. The pitch was successful, and the star player signed on with Northwood. Curtis continues:

> Transferring from [Division I to Division II], it was really important to her to know that she would have coaches who'd be willing to bend over backwards to help her succeed.

Since committing, she's been in the gym constantly with it. She's gotten the most shots up of any player on our team. She thinks it's the greatest thing in the world. So yeah, I think it's safe to say that ShotTracker had a very significant impact on her decision.[17]

ShotTracker can also be used during games, but it must be approved for use by the governing authority of the basketball organization in which it is being used. For example, in 2016 the National Association of Intercollegiate Athletics (NAIA) Men's Bas-

Because players are aware of analytics, schools that have them have an edge in recruiting. A star player could be drawn to a school with the latest tracking technology.

ketball National Championship allowed the use of ShotTracker during its annual tournament. As with Second Spectrum, Shot-Tracker was able to give coaches insights during the game that they could use during time-outs and halftime to make changes. One of those who did so was Kelly Wells, the head coach of the University of Pikeville in Kentucky. "Our offense is kind of spread out where [we] do a lot of dribble drives and things of that nature," explains Wells. "ShotTracker showed us the sweet spots where we were scoring. Being able to generate a lineup from that information became a critical piece of our strategy."[18]

College and high school teams now have access to technology that even the professionals did not have just a few years ago. Thanks to this technology, the generation of players now coming up through the ranks—men and women alike—are learning techniques that are more advanced than any used before. They are also practicing them with greater efficiency than ever before. In all likelihood, the skills of the next wave of players will make the professional leagues even more entertaining in the future.

CHAPTER FOUR

A Scientific Approach to Shooting

With 6.5 seconds left in the first game of the 2017 WNBA finals, the Minnesota Lynx led the Los Angeles Sparks by one point, 84–83. The Sparks had the ball out of bounds with time for one more play. Sparks forward Candace Parker made the inbound pass to guard Chelsea Gray, a three-year professional who had led the Sparks to the WNBA championship over the Lynx the year before. Receiving the ball well behind the three-point line, Gray drove hard to her left. With 3.7 seconds remaining on the clock, Gray pulled up at one of her favorite places to shoot, a spot on the court known as the left elbow, where the the free throw line meets the left boundary of the three-second lane, for a 16-foot (4.9 m), fall-away jump shot. A second later, the ball swished through the bottom of the net, giving the Sparks the lead and the game. "That is not an easy shot," former WNBA standout and ESPN basketball analyst Rebecca Lobo said to the play-by-play announcer Ryan Ruocco during a replay of the shot. "But Ryan, that's her sweet spot, and she got there. The left elbow—money!"[19]

Even under the extreme pressure of the championship series, Gray set her shooting arm perpendicular to the floor, with her elbow pointed at the basket—ideal mechanics for a game-winning "money" shot. It is the same technique that made Gray the league leader in three-point field goal percentage, averaging an incredible 48.2 percent from three-point range in 2017. Like other players rising through the college and professional ranks, Gray honed her technique using the latest science and technology.

Because scoring determines the outcome of a basketball game, shooting has attracted more scientific research than other areas of the sport. Dunks and layups are easy to understand, but outside shooting introduces many variables that have been examined. Not all experts agree on the science of shooting.

The Equipment

The object of shooting is to put the basketball through a metal hoop, or rim, that is 18 inches (46 cm) in diameter and located 10 feet (3 m) above the surface of the court. The rim is mounted on a rectangular backboard that measures 6 feet (1.8 m) wide and 3.5 feet (1.07 m) high. The backboard, which is usually made of tempered glass or Plexiglas, extends 33.75 inches (85.7 cm) above the rim and 8.25 inches (21 cm) below it. A rectangle measuring 24 inches (61 cm) horizontally and 18 inches (46 cm) vertically is outlined with a 2-inch (5 cm) band of white paint or otherwise marked on the backboard, centered on the basket. The bottom edge of the rectangle is located directly behind the rim, 10 feet (3 m) off the floor. The rectangle aids in the aiming of bank shots, shots that carom off the backboard and toward the rim.

The official NBA ball has a diameter from 9.43 to 9.51 inches (24 to 24.2 cm) and a circumference of 29.5 inches (75 cm). This is the same size ball used in men's college and high school basketball leagues. The official WNBA ball has a diameter of 9.07 inches (23 cm) and a circumference of 28.5 inches (72 cm). This ball is used for all women and girls ages twelve and up.

Entry Angle

The diameter of the ball is slightly more than half the diameter of the rim. That means if a ball is falling toward the rim from directly above, at a 90 degree angle from the floor, its path can deviate by as much as 4.5 inches (11.4 cm) off center in any direction and still pass through the hoop without touching it. The space left inside the rim after the basketball enters it is known as the hoop margin.

The only balls that can enter the basket from directly overhead, however, are those released by a player whose hands are above the rim or that bounce straight up off the rim and fall through the basket, like Don Nelson's buzzer-beating shot from 15 feet (4.6 m) with 1:33 left in the seventh game of the 1969 NBA finals that gave the Boston Celtics a 105–103 lead over the Los Angeles Lakers. This remarkable shot was chosen as one of the twenty-seven Top NBA Finals Moments in the league's seventy-year history. Nelson's shot descended at a 90-degree angle to the floor only because it had caromed off the back of the rim. Any shot that

The diameter of the ball is slightly more than half the diameter of the rim. The space left inside the rim after the basketball enters it is known as the hoop margin.

does not touch the rim and is not dropped from overhead by a player is descending toward the basket at an angle less than 90 degrees from the floor.

A shot descending at less than 90 degrees requires more of the available space inside the rim in order to fit through the opening. For example, if the basket were covered with a sheet of solid material, then a basketball falling from directly above could pass through a circular opening about 9.5 inches (24.1 cm) in diameter. This is because the top of the ball and the bottom of the ball are passing through the same location inside the hoop. However, a ball descending at any other angle could never pass through such a circle. It would always bounce out. This is because the bottom of the ball begins to enter the basket in one location, but because it takes time for the ball to pass through the hoop and the ball is moving forward as well as down, the top of the ball enters the hoop at a different location. Since the ball is falling at an angle, rather than straight down, it needs an oblong opening to enter the basket. The oblong shape takes up more of the room inside the basket, decreasing the hoop margin.

oblong
Deviating from a regular shape, such as a circular or square, by elongation in one dimension

The opening required for a ball to successfully enter the hoop is known as the apparent hoop size. A ball descending from a relatively high angle has a large apparent hoop size. A ball descending at a flatter angle has a smaller apparent hoop size, because its required opening is more oblong and takes up more of the basket's available space.

Since players can shoot the ball at different trajectories, the descending angles can change from shot to shot, and the apparent hoop size changes as well. According to researchers at Institut Supérieur du Sport et de l'Education Physique de Ksar-Said in Manouba, Tunisia, a ball released at a 60 degree angle will descend to the basket at a 53.51 degree angle. A ball released at a 52 degree angle will enter the hoop at a 41.37 degree angle. The ball released at 60 degrees has a larger apparent hoop size than the ball released at a 52 degree angle, so it has a better chance of going in. Because of his smaller size, Stephen Curry releases his jump shot at a 58.1 degree angle to get the ball over defenders. This is a higher trajectory than most NBA players use and gives Curry a larger apparent hoop size. It is one of the reasons why he is such an effective shooter.

trajectory
The path followed by a projectile flying or an object moving under the action of given forces

Velocity

The trajectory of a shot is not the only factor in effective shooting. Another important factor is the speed, or velocity, of the ball. A ball shot with a higher trajectory is falling toward the basket from a greater height. As a result, it is traveling faster when it reaches the rim than is a ball shot with a lower trajectory. For example, James Harden shoots with 49.6 degree launch angle. This means Harden's shot is falling from a lesser height and is traveling more slowly than Curry's shot is when it reaches the basket. As a result, Harden's shot lands more softly when his ball hits the rim, allowing it a better chance of falling into the basket. "Harden definitely has a 'shooter's touch' going for him because he is releasing with the optimum angle for the slowest moving ball as it nears the rim," writes Bob J. Fisher, author of *Straight Shooter: A Game-Changing New Approach to Basketball Shooting*. "However, Stephen Curry does not. Curry is opting for a larger target rather than a slow-moving ball as it nears the rim. The higher the launch angle, the larger the target area of the rim."[20]

The speed of the ball falling toward the rim is not the only velocity that affects shooting. The launch speed of the ball as it leaves the player's hand is also important. A ball traveling on a high arc to the basket needs to travel a greater distance than a shot at a lower trajectory does. To travel the greater distance, the ball must be launched with greater speed. This requires the shooter to apply more power to the shot, which can affect consistency.

Like other projectiles, a released basketball follows a U-shaped curving path known in mathematical terms as a parabola. Alan Marty, the founder and chair of Noah Basketball, which makes a system for automatically measuring the parabola of basketball shots, believes that 45 degrees is the ideal entry angle for a basketball shot. This is particularly true at the free throw line, where the shooter does not have to worry about getting the ball over a defender but instead needs the simplest and most repeatable shooting motion. Balls

parabola
A U-shaped curve in which any point on the curve is at an equal distance from a fixed point, known as the focus, and a fixed straight line, known as the directrix

Like other projectiles, a released basketball follows a U-shaped, curving path known in mathematical terms as a parabola. Some experts believe that 45 degrees is the ideal entry angle for a basketball shot.

descending from a greater height will have more speed due to gravity, and balls shot on a lower trajectory will require more speed to travel the distance.

By contrast, a ball launched near 45 degrees will be traveling at the slowest possible speed required to reach the rim, creating the softest possible landing and thereby increasing its chances of going in rather than bouncing off the rim. After measuring more than ten thousand shots by players of different skill levels, Marty concluded that a highly skilled shooter who shoots with a 45 degree arc makes an average of 96 percent of his or her free throws. An equally skilled shooter who uses a 53 degree arc makes 89 percent of the free throws, and a shooter with a 35 degree arc makes 80 percent of his or her free throws.

Tracking Shots in Real Time

Using this research, Marty helped build a machine that tracks the arc of a basketball shot and then immediately announces the angle of trajectory through a speaker system. The system uses a motion sensor placed 13 feet (4 m) above the rim that captures the position of the ball thirty times a second to map shots from their launch through the basket. This immediate feedback helps the shooter adjust the trajectory of his or her shot. The ideal score is forty-five, meaning a 45 degree entry angle. Dwayne Wade, a guard for the Miami Heat and tenth all-time scorer in NBA play-offs, turned to the device in the 2011–2012 season. The machine measured the arc of Wade's free throw entry angle at 40 degrees. Wade eventually was able to increase the arc of his shots, which led to more success at the free throw line. At the beginning of the season, Wade was making just 71 percent of his shots. After increasing the trajectory of his shots, he finished the season shooting 79 percent from the free throw line, the second-highest percentage of his career.

As with other computerized equipment, the Noah device gives coaches credibility that players are otherwise slow to give. "The biggest thing coaches say over and over is, 'Lift the ball, shoot it up,'" says John Welch, an assistant coach for the Denver Nug-

The Magnus Effect

When a basketball shooter releases the ball, it rolls off the fingers, creating backspin. This backspin works like a brake when the ball hits the rim or the backboard, deadening the bounce and improving the chances that the ball will carom into the basket. The backspin also allows the ball to travel slightly farther than it would if it had no spin, offsetting gravity by 1.5 percent. This is due to the Magnus effect, named after the nineteenth-century German physicist H.G. Magnus, who investigated the phenomenon in 1853. A spinning ball creates unequal pressure on the different sides of the ball, and this pressure causes the ball to curve. This curve can be seen in many different ball sports, including tennis, golf, baseball, and basketball.

The backspin imparted to the basketball causes the bottom edge of the ball to move faster through the air, due to the combined effect of the ball moving forward through the air and the rotating edge also moving forward toward the target. The air speed over the top edge of the ball is slower, because the surface is rotating the same direction as the air flow, which is away from the target. These unequal speeds means there is unequal friction against the surface of the ball—more friction at the bottom and less on the top. This creates unequal pressure on the ball, more from underneath and less from above. The added pressure from underneath creates a small amount of upward lift on the ball's trajectory, giving it a longer flight time.

gets. "We get tired of saying it; they get tired of hearing it. You can say it ten times and the ball flight doesn't change. They think they're lifting it but they're not. You put them on the Noah machine and they hear '39.' Well, their next shot is going to be 45. They react according to the objective data of Noah."[21]

Variety of Shots

The tagline for the Noah equipment is "Building the perfect arc," but not everyone agrees that a 45 degree entry angle is the perfect angle or that there even is such a thing as a perfect angle. "All players have different consistency in release angles and velocities," writes Irina Barzykina in her 2017 study "The Physics of an Optimal Basketball

Making a Free Throw

A free throw *should* be a sure thing but it is not. Professional players only succeed 75 percent of the time. So researchers have set out to determine the factors that are most likely to lead to a successful free throw. One of these factors is launch angle, or arc. The ideal launch angle is 52 degrees. This angle cuts down on velocity, which in turn reduces the chance of missing the basket because of a rebound. Another factor is backspin. The ideal backspin is 3 revolutions per second. At that rate, if the ball hits the rim or backboard, it slows down, stays closer to the basket, and is more likely to fall through the hoop. The final factor is aim. Many players aim for the center of the basket, but because few players have perfect aim, the ball often hits the front of the rim and drops straight down. The ideal target is 2.8 inches (7 cm) behind the center of the basket. Aiming between the backboard and the center of the hoop actually increases the chance of sinking the shot.

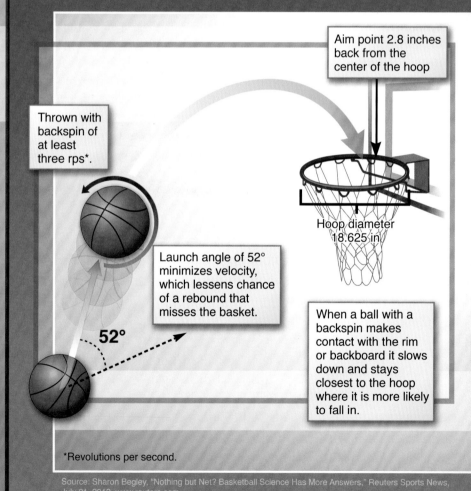

Aim point 2.8 inches back from the center of the hoop

Thrown with backspin of at least three rps*.

Hoop diameter 18.625 in

Launch angle of 52° minimizes velocity, which lessens chance of a rebound that misses the basket.

52°

When a ball with a backspin makes contact with the rim or backboard it slows down and stays closest to the hoop where it is more likely to fall in.

*Revolutions per second.

Source: Sharon Begley, "Nothing but Net? Basketball Science Has More Answers," Reuters Sports News, July 21, 2012. www.reuters.com.

Free Throw." She continues, "Some might need more space for error in velocity, and thus need a higher throwing angle, while others might aim lower because their velocity control is much stronger."[22]

John Fontanella, author of *The Physics of Basketball*, points out that the launch angle of a shot must vary depending on the height of the release point and the distance to the basket. For example, a shot released from 8 feet (2.4 m) above the court but a distance of only 2 feet (61 cm) in front of the rim must have a launch angle

The Perfect Free Throw

In the 1990s Larry M. Silverberg and Chau Tran, professors at North Carolina State University, developed a computer program to simulate the trajectories of millions of basketball shots. After two decades of research, Silverberg summarized the mathematics behind the "perfect" free throw:

We found that about 3 hertz [units of frequency per second] of backspin is the best amount; more than that does not help. It takes about 1 second for a ball to reach the basket, so 3 hertz equates to three revolutions in the air, from the instant the ball leaves the player's hands to when it reaches the basket.

Next, assuming the player releases the ball at 7 feet above the ground, a launch angle of about 52 degrees is best. In that angle, the launch speed is the lowest, and the probability of the shot being successful is the greatest. At 52 degrees, the shooter can be off a degree or more either way without a large effect on the shot's success. . . .

The last release condition was the most surprising: the aim point of the free throw. We found that the player should aim the ball to the back of the rim. Basically, the back of the rim is more forgiving than the front of the rim. At a release height of 7 feet, the gap between the ball and the back of the ring should be less than 2 inches. A small gap is best whether launching at low or high release heights.

Larry M. Silverberg, "The Math Behind the Perfect Free Throw," The Conversation, March 1, 2018. https://theconversation.com.

of at least 72 degrees to clear the rim. As the shooter moves away from the rim, the launch angle can decrease. Fontanella states that the slowest moving, or ideal, shot from the free throw line, 15 feet (4.6 m) from the basket, is 51 degrees. From three-point range, the ideal trajectory is 45 degrees. Fontanella also notes that the ideal launch angle from the free throw line varies depending on the player's height and the resulting height of the shot release. For example, Fontanella says that a 5-foot-4-inch (163 cm) player should launch the ball at a 52.2 degree angle, a 5-foot-8-inch (173 cm) player at a 51.5 degree angle, a 6-foot (183 cm) player at a 50.8 degree angle, and a 7-foot (213 cm) player a 48.7 degree angle.

Many shooting coaches believe the ideal shot should swish through the net without touching the rim. Although the swish is an aesthetically pleasing shot, John Carter, chief executive officer of Noah Basketball, does not believe it is the most effective one. He points out that the back of the rim works as a kind of backboard for shots, allowing the shooter to overshoot the center of the basket and still make the shot. Noah tracking equipment has revealed that the ideal point for shooters to aim at is not in the center of the basket, but 11 inches (28 cm) beyond the front of the rim, or 2 inches (5 cm) past the center of the basket. "Many players today simply do not shoot the ball deep enough in the basket," says Carter. "You don't get an extra point for a swish. The research clearly finds that players who shoot the ball deeper in the basket make more shots. Watch some of the best shooters, and you'll see they don't always swish the ball. Instead, they often hit the back of the rim and score a BRAD shot, which stands for 'Back Rim And Down.'"[23]

Science and technology are already improving the range and accuracy of shooting. As technology advances, engineers will continue to find ways to track the flight of the ball and communicate that information to athletes who seek to improve their shooting skills. Improved shooting will put an even greater pressure on defenders to disrupt the shooters' rhythm and force them to take shots from places where they are not as likely to make shots—a practice that will likely be aided by technology as well.

CHAPTER FIVE

Applying Technology to Physical Training

Basketball is widely considered the most physically demanding of all team sports. Unlike football, basketball requires players to play both offense and defense and to switch from one to the other instantaneously. There are no natural breaks in the flow of the game; players race from one end of the court to the other in constant motion. Unlike baseball, in which players on both offense and defense usually run forward in straight lines or gentle arcs, basketball requires players to run forward, backward, and side to side, changing directions in the blink of an eye. Basketball players must be able to stop and accelerate quickly; jump high to shoot, defend, and rebound; and be strong enough to battle for position under the basket. At the same time, basketball requires excellent hand-eye coordination, especially when shooting and passing. And unlike baseball and all individual sports except for boxing, basketball requires the players to perform all of the required skills with at least one defensive player trying to stop them. "Basketball is the most demanding sport we've invented," wrote Bill Russell, the Hall of Fame center who led the Boston Celtics to eleven world championships during his thirteen years as a professional player. "It demands speed and stamina and a lot of other physical and mental qualities."[24]

Tracking Fitness

To meet the many physical and mental demands of basketball, even naturally gifted athletes must train. For example, to build stamina, athletes must exercise the heart and lungs to increase the efficiency with which they supply oxygen to the muscles. This cardiovascular exercise does not have to occur in the gym or even be directly related to basketball. Running, biking, swimming, and rowing can all improve cardiovascular efficiency. The key is to raise the heart rate for long periods of time—beyond the endurance needed to play a basketball game. This added amount of endurance gives the player stamina in the late stages of the game, when the outcome is often decided.

cardiovascular
Of, relating to, or involving the heart and blood vessels

Swimming, running, and biking can all improve cardiovascular efficiency. The key is to raise the heart rate for long periods of time to build the endurance needed to play a full basketball game.

To measure their progress in stamina training, players often wear lightweight waterproof wristbands, such as the Garmin Vivosmart 4 or Fitbit Alta HR, that collect physiological metrics such as heart rate and blood oxygen levels. Fitness trackers can be paired with cell phone apps to measure fitness progress, create new fitness goals, and design workouts to increase stamina. These devices usually do not have a Global Positioning System (GPS) device inside, so they must be paired with the user's cell phone to track distances traveled during a workout. However, some sports watches, such as Polar Vantage M, the Garmin Forerunner 235, and even the Apple Watch, do have a built-in GPS to go along with their biometric data capturing.

biometric
Relating to or involving the application of statistical analysis to biological data

At the high-priced end of fitness trackers is WHOOP, which is worn by several NBA stars, including LeBron James and Kyle Lowry, a guard for the Toronto Raptors. The device has five embedded sensors that constantly monitor and track heart rate, heart rate variability, ambient temperature, motion, and skin conductivity from the wearer's wrist. It takes these readings hundreds of times a second and stores the data to be accessed with a smartphone application. Using this data, the app can not only track activity, it can calculate the speed of recovery after a workout or game, the overall strain of a day's exercise, and sleep quality. The device's strain score is displayed on a scale from 0 to 21, with 0 to 9 being light, 10 to 14 being moderate, 14 to 18 being strenuous, and 18 to 21 being all out. The device tracks three metrics while the wearer sleeps—heart rate variability, resting heart rate, and hours of sleep—and uses this data to calculate the athlete's recovery, or readiness for activity, in the morning. "WHOOP showed me how my recovery affected my shooting and free-throw percentage . . . even my turnovers," says Lowry. "That blew me away."[25]

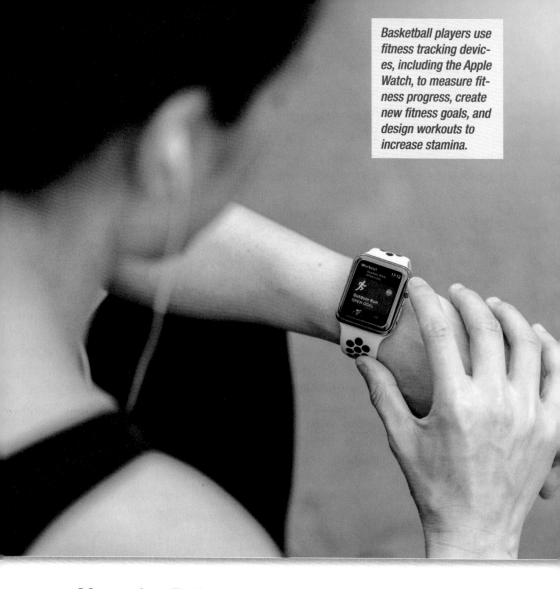

Measuring Fatigue

With its many rapid starts, stops, and changes of direction and all its running and jumping, basketball puts more stress on more parts of the body than any other sport. Injuries are common. Professional teams and elite college programs are using technology to reduce injuries. Twelve NBA teams have their players wear fitness trackers during practice so they can analyze how well or poorly an athlete is moving, compared to that player's history. This analysis is designed for teams to identify when a player is fatigued, since tired players are more prone to injury. Teams have preset parameters for what they consider to be a player's danger zone for fatigue. If the player meets these criteria, the coach will rest the player accordingly. "A lot of non-contact injuries are fatigue-related," explains Keke Lyles, director of athletic performance for the Golden State Warriors, a team that requires players to wear wristbands from Catapult Sports in practice.

parameter
A boundary or limit

> If we see big drops consistently over the last few games, and we know in practice they've dropped and they're telling us they're tired and sore and beat up, then we start painting a big picture: 'Yeah, these guys are probably fatigued.' When they're fatigued, they're at a higher risk.[26]

Fans are disappointed when they purchase tickets to a game, only to find that a star player is being rested. However, Magic Johnson says resting players is vital to a team's long-term success. "Safety is important, because we are paying these players a couple hundred million dollars and we want them around for a long time," says Johnson. Wearable technology helps the team know when a player might be at risk of injury. "I think it's going to help us to really monitor a young man in terms of his practice time and keeping him safe," says Johnson. "We can't keep him from getting injured, but if we have enough information, he probably won't be injured as much."[27]

Sleep is an important part of an athlete's recovery, and some NBA teams are using technology to maximize sleep efficiency. For example, the Dallas Mavericks have partnered with the bedding company Bedgear, which has also designed sleep solutions for the National Football League's Denver Broncos and Major League Baseball's Boston Red Sox, to create a personalized sleep system for Mavericks players. Bedgear uses textiles that keep pillows at a cool temperature and fabrics that eliminate moisture, both of which promote sound sleep. Pillows vary in size, thickness, and firmness, and they are matched to the athletes' body frame and sleeping habits, including whether they sleep on their backs, sides, or stomachs. The goal is to have the athlete sleep in one position for as long as possible. A person who tosses and turns during sleep will not recover as completely as one who remains more or less in one place throughout the night. "We are always looking for innovators that will help enhance the Mavs performance—whether it's physical, mental or some combination of both," says Mavericks owner Mark Cuban. "Sleep is such an important part of an athlete's life, especially when we travel and have back-to-back games, and I'm excited to see how the guys react to the products and program."[28]

Tracking Vertical Leaps

Athletes and coaches are also using technology to enhance specific skills used in basketball, such as jumping and dribbling. Jumping is an action that requires specific technique in order to produce maximum effects. Greater pressure against the ground results in higher jumps. Greater ground pressure is a combination of factors, including muscle strength, muscle involvement, and the amount the knee is bent. Force platforms or force plates are measuring instruments that measure the ground reaction forces generated by a body standing on or moving across them. Force plates calculate the height of the jump based on the jumper's power output, the angle of the jump, and the time the athlete spends in the air.

A new generation of wearables also measures jump performance. These devices contain motion sensors that are paired with cell phone apps to accurately measure jump height and give immediate feedback to the athlete. One of these devices is the Vert tracking system. The Vert sensor attaches to the clothing of the athlete and sends motion information about a jump to a cell phone app that interprets the data. The app measures the jumper's initial velocity and landing impact and makes more than fifty calculations to measure the upward movement of the jumper's center of mass, a point located around the hip area. The equipment is able to calculate the vertical height of a jump with 96 percent accuracy. The

Wearable Technology Improves Shooting

According to *USA Today*, almost 16 percent of NBA finals games and 17 percent of NCAA tournament games since 1952 have been won by one or two points. As a result, coaches are always searching for ways to increase their scoring, even if it is only by a point or two. One of the first places coaches look to improve is at the free throw line, where players have uncontested shots. Coaches at the University of Maryland (UMD) turned to a new technology to see whether they could increase their team's free throw shooting. They outfitted their players with the SOLIDshot sleeve, which gives immediate feedback about the arm position and release point while shooting.

UMD tested the equipment by letting half of the players use it during practice and the other half not. The players who practiced with the SOLIDshot sleeve saw an average increase of 12 percent in their free throw shooting during actual games, versus an average increase of 4 percent among players who practiced without SOLIDshot. Overall, team free throw shooting improved by 6 percent. "SOLIDshot really helped our players shoot with confidence," says UMD basketball head coach Mark Turgeon. "Our free throw percentage went up six-percent as a team, which helped us win many close games."

Quoted in SOLIDshot, "Case Study: University of Maryland Men's Basketball," 2018. www.solidshot.com.

landing data is important as well, because it lets the jumper know when he or she is landing too hard in a way that could result in wear and tear on the joints and ultimately lead to an injury.

Measuring from the center of mass is more accurate than mechanical systems, such as the Vertec "slapstick." Vertec consists of a pole with horizontal vanes that the jumper strikes with his or her hand at the peak of the jump. The vanes rotate out of the way when they are struck, indicating the height the jumper reached. Vertec cannot provide data about landing force, and its results must be noted by hand. By contrast, the Vert app not only stores data but offers statistical context, such as which jump is the highest in a session, how a jump compares to the athlete's best all-time jump, the average height of the top twenty-five jumps in a session, and how that average compares to previous sessions. The system also tracks the number of jumps in a session, primarily as a way to prevent overexertion and injury. As with other training devices, the immediate feedback of an electronic jumping system helps the athlete build "muscle memory" for how the best jumps feel.

Another jump tracking device, Blast Motion, adds visual flair to the data collection. Like Vert, Blast Motion pairs a motion sensor that is attached to the athlete's clothing with a cell phone app. It tracks the player's acceleration, jump height, hang time, and rotation in the air. It keeps a history of the measurements, but its unique feature is its ability to sync up with a cell phone's video camera to create clips of the key performances. The replay system automatically trims and assigns the video to the event tracked by the sensor, creating what is essentially a highlight video of the athlete's best efforts or plays. The replay system automatically overlays the video with metrics captured by the sensor, so the athlete can see when a jump reached its peak, how much he or she rotated in the air, and so forth. The viewer watches the video frame by frame for detailed analysis of what happened during the jump. This visual feedback is available immediately, so a player can work on improving the move.

Technology to Improve Shooting

Technology is also helping coaches and players analyze and improving shooting. Optical tracking systems such as Second Spectrum, SportVU, and Noah Basketball, as well as systems with embedded sensors in the ball, such as ShotTracker, help coaches and players track not only the arc of shots but also their direction. These systems reveal whether shooters consistently miss on one side or another or whether their shots are too long or come up short. When coaches understand where a player misses shots, they know what to correct in the player's shooting mechanics. "ShotTracker is a huge innovation for the sport of basketball," says Golden State Warriors guard Klay Thompson,

Players like LeBron James are taking longer shots with greater accuracy than anyone who ever played before. Advantages created by new science and technology will continue to improve player performance.

who uses the system. "Repetition, accountability and confidence make great shooters, and ShotTracker delivers all three."[29]

Sporting goods giant Wilson and a company called 94Fifty both make a ball with an embedded sensor to help individual players improve their shooting. The sensor sends information about the shooter's release speed and the ball's arc and backspin to the user's cell phone via Bluetooth technology. An accompanying app processes the information and provides it to the shooter

Technology Helps Develop Dribbling Skills

Dribbling effectively is vital to penetrating defenses. "You can't go anywhere, you can't create any type of space between yourself and a defender if you can't handle the basketball," says Britnea Moore, a certified basketball trainer who was a standout guard at California State University, Monterey Bay. In her classes, Moore uses the DribbleUp smart basketball, a training aid that is different from basketballs designed to improve shooting.

Instead of having embedded sensors, the DribbleUp ball is designed with a pattern imprinted on the surface that allows a cell phone camera to track its motion. The ball otherwise looks and feels like a normal basketball, and it can be used for shooting and playing just like any other ball. But when the player works on dribbling in front of the cell phone, which is held by a stand at floor level, the app is able to track the ball's motion precisely. The app in the phone displays metrics such as dribble speed, hesitation, and speed of a move—such as a crossover dribble—in real time. The app features a thermometer-type meter on the side of the screen that gives live feedback on dribble speed. "If that meter isn't up into the green area, you kind of push yourself to get it there," says Moore. The app includes a thirty-day guided training program that provides the user with drills designed to improve the player's ball handling skills and gives voice coaching as the player performs the drills.

Quoted in Jonathan Bloom, "High-Tech Basketball Could Help You Handle Like the Pros," ABC-7 News, June 7, 2017. https://abc7news.com.

in real time. The app also gives both voice and on-screen coaching tips. "I could actually play and get the verbal feedback right in my ear with every shot," says Fritz Nelson, a product reviewer for LiveScience who tried out 94Fifty. "I got not only a score, but also adjustment tips from a coach's voice after each shot: 'Bend those legs;' 'point your elbow;' 'flick your wrist.' In most cases, I realized it truly did know what I'd done wrong."[30]

Another piece of high-tech equipment focuses on the shooter instead of the ball. The SOLIDshot basketball smart sleeve is a wearable device that fits over the player's shooting arm and uses three embedded sensors—one on a player's bicep, another on the forearm, and a third on the hand—to record fifty metrics during the shot. The motion is captured and analyzed to give real-time feedback on shooting mechanics. The sleeve produces sounds to indicate when the player has executed a good shot. In January 2016 the Detroit Pistons turned to SOLIDshot to help the team's two-time all-star center, Andre Drummond, improve his free throw shooting. At the time, Drummond was shooting a dismal 34.7 percent from the line. Three months later, by the end of the season, he had raised his average to 35.5 percent. His average rose again in 2017, to 38.6 percent. By the 2018 season, he was making 60.5 percent of his free throws. "So now he has the feedback that my elbow is creeping out," says Pistons coach Stan Van Gundy says. "That's why we're looking at this thing because it can give him more than just keep your elbow in. He can really look and see."[31]

Athletic performance is determined not just by talent and skill levels but also by physical fitness. Technology is playing a greater role than ever in the training that develops physical fitness and reduces injuries. Today's athletes are the product of more than natural ability. They are in many ways being physically engineered to perform specific athletic tasks with greater ability than ever before. Players like Stephen Curry, James Harden, and LeBron James are taking longer shots with greater accuracy than anyone who ever played before. Both the NBA and WNBA have seen many great players in the past, but because of advantages being created by science and technology, their greatest stars are likely yet to come.

SOURCE NOTES

Introduction: Beyond Statistics

1. Quoted in Joe Lemire, "Warriors, Sportradar, ShotTracker Discuss the State of Basketball Analytics," SportTechie, October 22, 2018. www.sporttechie.com.
2. Euan Hunter, "How Technology Is Impacting Basketball," Innovation Enterprise, October 12, 2018. https://channels .theinnovationenterprise.com.

Chapter One: The Biomechanics of Basketball

3. Quoted in David Fleming, "Sports' Perfect 0.4 Seconds," ESPN, April 1, 2014. www.espn.com.
4. Mike Reinold, "Strength Training for Runners," MikeReinold. com, December, 2018. https://mikereinold.com.
5. Quoted in National Basketball Association, "Final 3:39 of Game 7 of the 2016 NBA Finals: Cavaliers vs Warriors," YouTube, December 24, 2016. www.youtube.com /watch?v=wgVOgGLtPtc.

Chapter Two: Mapping the Game

6. Quoted in Mia Jackson, "Big Data Becoming as Important as Scouting and Just as Closely Guarded," Global Sport Matters, August 8, 2018. https://globalsportmatters.com.
7. Quoted in Daniel Terdiman, "How the NBA Became the World's Most Tech-Savvy Sports League," *Fast Company*, June 9, 2017. www.fastcompany.com.
8. Kirk Goldsberry, "The Harden Experience Is Unprecedented and Undeniable," ESPN, January 9, 2019. http://tv5.espn .com.

Chapter Three: Making Practice More Effective

9. Quoted in Bill Plaschke, "A Grateful Dad Passes It Along," *Los Angeles Times*, March 21, 2002. www.latimes.com.
10. Quoted in SVG Staff, "Duke Basketball Deploys Big-Data Analytics," Sports Video Group News, April 20, 2015. www.sportsvideo.org.
11. Quoted in ShotTracker, "How TCU Uses Live Analytics to Drive Competition in Practice," 2018. https://shottracker.com.
12. Quoted in ShotTracker, "How TCU Uses Live Analytics to Drive Competition in Practice."
13. Quoted in ShotTracker, "How TCU Uses Live Analytics to Drive Competition in Practice."
14. Quoted in ShotTracker, "How to Solve the Recruiting Puzzle with Live Analytics," 2018. https://shottracker.com.
15. Quoted in ShotTracker, "How to Solve the Recruiting Puzzle with Live Analytics."
16. Quoted in ShotTracker, "Mike Brey—Coaching with Analytics," 2018. https://shottracker.com.
17. Quoted in ShotTracker, "How to Solve the Recruiting Puzzle with Live Analytics."
18. Quoted in ShotTracker, "Powering the Future of Competition," 2018. https://shottracker.com.

Chapter Four: A Scientific Approach to Shooting

19. Rebecca Lobo, "Chelsea Gray's CLUTCH Shot Wins WNBA Finals Game 1!," YouTube, September 24, 2017. www.youtube.com/watch?v=lp45FXpoO8k.
20. Bob J. Fisher, *Straight Shooter: A Game-Changing New Approach to Basketball Shooting*. Dublin, OH: Telemachus, 2018, p. 130.
21. Quoted in Jordan Schultz, "The Science of Swish: Basketball Coaches, Players Search 'Perfect' Shot," *Huffington Post*, May 10, 2012. www.huffingtonpost.com.

22. Irina Barzykina, "The Physics of an Optimal Basketball Free Throw," ResearchGate, February 2017. www.researchgate .net.

23. Quoted in Michael Austin, "Building the Perfect Arc in Your Shot," Winning Hoops, 2019. https://winninghoops.com.

Chapter Five: Applying Technology to Physical Training

24. William F. Russell, "I'm Not Involved Anymore," *Sports Illustrated*, August 4, 1968, p. 17.

25. Quoted in Mark Van Deusen, "Who Takes the Big Shot?," WHOOP, November 29, 2016. www.whoop.com.

26. Quoted in Ken Berger, "Warriors 'Wearable' Weapon? Devices to Monitor Players While on the Court," CBS Sports, June 3, 2015. www.cbssports.com.

27. Quoted in ShotTracker, "Magic Johnson Talks ShotTracker," 2018. https://shottracker.com.

28. Quoted in Kendra Andrews, "Dallas Mavericks Partner with Bedgear's Sleep Experts for Performance Bedding," *Sports Illustrated*, October 13, 2016. www.si.com.

29. Quoted in My Nguyen, "The Best Wearable Devices for Basketball," Wearable Technologies, October 9, 2015. www .wearable-technologies.com.

30. Fritz Nelson, "94Fifty Smart Sensor Basketball Review," LiveScience, February 14, 2014. www.livescience.com.

31. Quoted in Ananth Pandian, "Andre Drummond Turning to Technology to Improve Free Throws," CBS Sports, January 28, 2016. www.cbssports.com.

FOR FURTHER RESEARCH

Books

Dorian Bohler, *Physics & Basketball*. Laptop Lifestyle, 2017.

Bob J. Fisher, *Straight Shooter: A Game-Changing New Approach to Basketball Shooting*. Dublin, OH: Telemachus, 2018.

Jerry V. Krause and Craig Nelson, *Basketball Skills & Drills*. Champaign, IL: Human Kinetics, 2019.

Alexandru Radu, ed., *The Science of Basketball*. New York: Routledge, 2018.

Angie Smibert, *STEM in Basketball*. Minneapolis, MN: ABDO, 2018.

Internet Sources

George Anadiotis, "NBA Analytics and RDF Graphs: Game, Data, and Metadata Evolution, and Occam's Razor," ZDNet, June 7, 2018. www.zdnet.com.

Andy Frye, "New Tech in Basketball May Give Teams More of an Edge," *Forbes*, May 16, 2018. www.forbes.com.

Kirk Goldsberry, "The Harden Experience Is Unprecedented and Undeniable," ESPN, January 9, 2019. http://tv5.espn.com.

Danielle Rose, "Biomechanics of the Basketball Jump Shot," *Biomechanical Principles of a Jump Shot* (blog), June 19, 2016. http://daniellerosehlpe3531.blogspot.com.

Carvell Wallace, "Stephen Curry and the Warriors' Astonishing Season," *New Yorker*, May 31, 2016. www.newyorker.com.

Websites

NBA Advanced Stats (https://stats.nba.com). The world's premiere professional basketball league makes both traditional statistics—most points, most rebounds, most assists—and statistics captured and processed by its optical tracking system available to the public on this website. The advanced statistics includes metrics such as player impact estimate, offensive rating, defensive rating, and field goal efficiency.

NCAA Men's Basketball (www.ncaa.org/sports/mens-basketball). The home page of men's college basketball has information about all three league levels—Division I, Division II, and Division III. Division I alone consists of 353 teams in thirty-two conferences. Scores, standings, and traditional statistics are all featured.

NCAA Women's Basketball (www.ncaa.org/sports/womens-basketball). The home page of women's college basketball offers news about teams, players, and trends. All three divisions are represented in the menu, with statistics for each one.

Women's National Basketball Association (www.wnba.com). The official website of the WNBA offers team and player information and videos. The website offers traditional statistics as well as some advanced statistics, including effective field goal percentage, usage percentage, and player impact estimate.

INDEX

Korver, Kyle, 29–30

Lacob, Kirk, 6
levers, 21
Lobo, Rebecca, 44
Los Angeles Clippers, 28, 31–32
Los Angeles Sparks, 44
Lowe, Zach, 26
Lowry, Kyle, 57
Lyles, Keke, 59

Magnus, H.G., 51
Magnus effect, 51
Marquette University, 33–34
Marshall, Clif, 31
Marty, Alan, 49, 50
Milwaukee Bucks, 29
Minnesota Lynx, 44
Mitchell, Donovan, 15
Mocap Analytics, 6
momentum, definition of, 14
Moneyball (film), 22
Montigel, Thomas, 35, 37–38, 39
Moore, Britnea, 64

National Basketball
   Association (NBA), 6
   fastest runners in, 15
   greatest jumpers in, 20
National Collegiate Athletic
   Association (NCAA),
   optical tracking in, 31,
   33–34

NBA Advanced Stats
   (website), 70
NCAA. *See* National
   Collegiate Athletic
   Association
NCAA Men's Basketball
   (website), 70
NCAA Women's Basketball
   (website), 70
Nelson, Don, 46
Nelson, Fritz, 64
Noah Basketball, 49, 50–51
Nowitzki, Dirk, 24

Oakland Athletics, 22
oblong, definition of, 47
one-legged jumps, 13–15
optical, definition of, 6
optical tracking analysis,
   24–27, 62–65
   cost of, 33
   use by NCAA, 31, 33–34

parabola, 49
parameter, definition of, 59
Parker, Candace, 17, 44
"Physics of an Optimal
   Basketball Free Throw,
   The" (Barzykina), 51, 53
Physics of Basketball, The
   (Fontanella), 53–54
Polar Vantage M (sports
   watch), 57
predictive analysis, definition
   of, 22

PICTURE CREDITS

ABOUT THE AUTHOR

Bradley Steffens is a poet, a novelist, and an award-winning author of more than fifty nonfiction books for children and young adults.